Countries

Egypt

by Christine Juarez

raintree

a Capstone company — publishers for children

Raintree is an imprint of Capstone Global Library Limited, a company incorporated in England and Wales having its registered office at 264 Banbury Road, Oxford, OX2 7DY – Registered company number: 6695582

www.raintree.co.uk
myorders@raintree.co.uk

Edited by Erika L. Shores
Designed by Bobbie Nuytten
Picture research by Tracy Cummins
Production by Laura Manthe

Printed in China
ISBN 978 1 4747 1978 0
20 19 18 17 16
10 9 8 7 6 5 4 3 2 1

British Library Cataloguing in Publication Data
A full catalogue record for this book is available from the British Library.

Photo Credits
Alamy: Simon Reddy, 13; Newscom: David Rogers Africapictures.net, 11, MOHAMED OMAR/EPA, 14, Oliviero Olivieri/ Robert Harding, 17; Shutterstock: Baloncici, 19, Enrico Montanari, 7, Ivsanmas, 4, Mikael Damkier, 5, mrHanson, 9, Ohmega1982, back cover (globe), RYGER, cover, 1 (design element), sculpies, 1, Vladimir Wrangel, 22 (flag), Winiki, 22 (currency), WitR, cover, 21

We would like to thank Gail Saunders-Smith, Ph.D., for her invaluable help in the preparation of this book.

Note to Parents and Teachers

The Countries series supports learning related to people, places and culture. This book describes and illustrates Egypt. The images support early readers in understanding the text. The repetition of words and phrases helps early readers learn new words. This book also introduces early readers to subject-specific vocabulary, which is defined in the Glossary section. Early readers may need assistance to read some words and to use the Contents, Glossary, Read more, Websites and Index sections of the book.

Contents

Where is Egypt?

Egypt is a country in north-east Africa. It is almost twice as big as France. Egypt's capital city is Cairo.

Cairo★

EGYPT

5

Landforms

Deserts are Egypt's main landforms.

The Western Desert is part

of the huge Sahara Desert.

The Arabian Desert lies

in eastern Egypt.

1

Animals

Egypt's wild animals live in deserts or along the River Nile. Snakes and lizards hide under rocks. Birds, such as herons, storks and cranes, eat fish from the Nile.

heron

Language and population

More than 85 million people live in Egypt. Just over half the population lives in crowded cities. The other half lives in rural areas. Egyptians speak Arabic.

Food

Meals including bread and beans
are common in Egypt.
Egyptians eat stewed fava beans
almost every day. They call
this dish *fuul*.

Celebrations

Most Egyptians are Muslims who follow Islam. Muslims celebrate Eid al-Fitr to mark the end of Ramadan. Ramadan is a time of fasting.

15

Where people work

Half of Egypt's people have service jobs. These jobs include teaching, banking and selling. Outside the cities, most people farm. Farmers grow cotton, rice and corn.

Transportation

Egyptians can travel in many ways. Roads and railways join cities. People use buses, trains, cars and bikes. Donkeys and camels are used outside cities.

19

Famous sight

Egyptians built huge pyramids over 4,500 years ago. They buried Egyptian kings inside them. The largest pyramid is about 137 metres (450 feet) tall.

Country facts

Name: Egypt

Capital: Cairo

Population: 85,294,388 (July 2013 estimate)

Size: 1,001,450 square kilometres (386,662 square miles)

Language: Arabic

Main crops: cotton, rice, corn, beans, fruit

Egypt's flag

Money: Egyptian pound

Glossary

capital city in a country where the government is based

celebrate do something fun on a special day

crane large wading bird with long legs and a long neck and bill

desert dry area with little rain

fava bean large, flattened seed of a fava plant

heron bird with a long, thin beak and long legs

landform natural feature of the land

language words used in a particular country or by a particular group of people

Muslim person who follows the religion of Islam; Islam is based on the teachings of the prophet Muhammad

population group of people living in the same place

pyramid large, stone structure used long ago to bury Egyptian kings

Ramadan Islamic religious holiday when Muslims fast

rural to do with the countryside

stork large bird with long, thin legs and a thin neck; storks wade in water

Read more

Ancient Egypt (History Detective Investigates), Rachel Minay (Wayland, 2014)

Egypt: A Benjamin Blog and His Inquisitive Dog Guide (Country Guides), Anita Ganeri (Raintree, 2015)

Websites

ngkids.co.uk/history/ten-facts-about-ancient-egypt
Learn more about Egypt with these fascinating facts.

www.bbc.co.uk/history/ancient/egyptians
Discover cool facts about hieroglyphs, mummification, gods and goddesses.

Index